ARMATURE

ARMATURE
CHRISSIE GITTINS

PUBLICATIONS
2003

Published by Arc Publications
Nanholme Mill, Shaw Wood Road
Todmorden, Lancs OL14 6DA

Design by Tony Ward
Printed by Antony Rowe Ltd.,
Eastbourne, East Sussex

ISBN 1 900072 70 X

Acknowledgments:
Some of the poems in this collection have
appeared in, or been broadcast on:
As Girls Could Boast (Oscars Press, 1994); *Bangkok Patana Update;*
BBC Radio Four; BBC World Service; *Creative Writing* by Julia
Casterton (Macmillan, 1998); *The Cutting Room; Envoi; Fatchance;*
The Insider (HMP Maidstone); *The Interpreter's House; The Kent
Messenger; Looking Beyond the Brochure* (Tourism Concern); *Magma;
The Observer; Odyssey; Orbis; Poems are Private* (Pearson Education,
2001); *Poems '91 Lancaster Literature Festival; Poetry News; Poetry
Street N16; Poetry Wales; Reactions 3* (Pen&inc, 2002); *The Rialto;
Smiths Knoll; Staple; Thumbscrew; Tourism in Focus.*

A number of these poems appeared in two pamphlet collections
published by Dagger Press:
A Path of Rice (1997), and *Pilot* (2001).

'Archangel' was a runner-up in the Manchester Open competition,
1994. 'L'Usage de la Parole' won the Poet and Artist competition
in Poetry News 1994. 'Psyche's Moan' was commended in the
1995 Greenwich Festival competition. 'No Further' was a prize-
winner in the Yorkshire Open, 1996. 'The Glass Mountain' was a
prizewinner in the 1997 Poetry News competition. 'The Borrowed
House' was a prizewinner in the 2002 Poetry News 'Fire' compe-
tition. 'Armature' was a runner-up in the Ottakar's Faber Poetry
Competition 2002. 'Taking Alice to the New British Library' was
written during a Poetry Society Poetry Place with the Refugee
Council in 1999 and broadcast on the BBC World Service. 'Yalding.
15th October 2000,' and 'Thoughts of a Man in Maidstone Jail'
were commissioned by Maidstone Borough Council while the au-
thor was Writer-in-Residence there 2000-2001.

Thanks are due to the Oppenheim-John Downes Memorial Trust
for an award in 1998, to Hawthornden Castle for a fellowship in
2001 and to the Society of Authors and the Royal Literary Fund
for their generous support.

The publishers acknowledge financial assistance
from the Arts Council of England, Yorkshire.

Editor UK & Ireland: Jo Shapcott

for the Karenni
and all my families

CONTENTS

A PATH OF RICE

PILOT

TODAY IS FRIDAY, THE SEASON IS WINTER, THE WEATHER IS COLD

but a lemon hangs from a branch in the conservatory.
You sit with the men at tables on the right,
away from the white-haired ladies,
waiting to be served a sandwich from a tray.
I hold your gaze till I appear in your vision,
your hands rise to mine.

We have been hearing
that you're dressed correctly for the time of year,
that you dress in the correct order –
though Mum helped this morning
to take pyjamas from beneath a vest;
a '*once a day man*,' your keyworker says,
'*good control*,' '*loves to sing*,'
as you sit with the incontinent of mind,
prompted by staff with clues to the daily crossword puzzle.

We take you home, you chirrup all the way –
'*My father went to school down here*',
'*Take this turning on the right*',
bent and hunched you help Mum from the car.

The past is still within your grasp,
it's the present which gives you jip.
You stand too long next to a chair –
defying it to seat you,
food evades your fork,
pasta bows give chase around your plate,
'*navilla*' ice-cream billows from its dish.

In the morning, you're sitting diligently on your bedroom chair,
heaped over Yellow Pages,
looking for a number we no longer need.
You complain about our diction –

we repeat words over and over.
I wait for the rain before stepping to the car,
I've distracted you from the washing machine –
it's tiresome sticking door,
your last word to me is '*Pardon?*'

Your hand, curled like a sepal,
waves from side to side through the blank window.

PILOT

How was it I could still smell the lilies from the kitchen window sill
when I woke from a nap in a service station,
or as I drove between three warning chevrons?
Before I left, the moors were painted with a peach wash
as the sun sank in the sky.
I drove away from clusters of stone cottages,
mullioned windows, your home surrounded
by hog's back hills
to a city I cannot see across,
whose river severs north from south,
whose skies are boxed with sloping rooves.

You left your home by ambulance
requesting two eggs for breakfast as you arrived
feet first at Casualty,
dragged from your own bed
and the sounds you understood.
Only the day before, you said
there was another life still to live –
you would like to have been a pilot.
While I stroked the baby bowl of your forehead
you folded in and out of pain.

Sitting in the hospital bed
your clean pyjamas didn't quite fasten
over the buttonhole of your navel,
the crackle glaze of veins in your cheek
ran down your neck
to meet the thin white path of your by-pass scar.
Sitting in an upright chair you thought the bed a body bag,
its thick green cover hugged a waning mattress.

You were afraid of the figures
moving around the end of the ward.
They were silent and invisible to me.

THERE ARE THINGS I MUST REALIZE
YOU CAN NO LONGER DO

There are things I must realize you can no longer do –
climb the hill that was the view from your window
where we've climbed and talked of the past,
eat with a familiar wooden handled spoon,
sleep in that narrow bed pushed hard against the wall.

Now this corridor contains your wandering,
or you are wedged into a chair with a hospital trolley.
There are no doors in your mind to say
this is a true story, that is not.
A nurse can talk about your inconsistency
whilst wearing perfect make-up.
A doctor wants to know if you can pay for your care.

From the mercury rush of your words
there are still some stones to gather –
'*You'll have a good drink of coffee before you go?*
Make a sandwich – you can get them pre-wrapped now.'
'*I always wanted to protect you.*'

The veins in your hands stretch like a washing line
pegged with the sheet of your skin.
The man in the opposite bed is wearing your watch.

'N'

The first two shops had 'T's' embroidered in white
and 'M' in royal blue,
'N' took three shops to find.

An empty carousel of yellow ponies
spun through the rain.
The Sally Army played bright carols in the square.

I found your three handkerchiefs rolled in their box like bolsters,
hanging between the socks and serried ties.
They were what you'd asked for.

Will these flat stitches ensure they stay in your room?
Or will they join the chain of chattels
passing between each patient?
You have so little of your own –
a geranium,
a poster of a biplane,
a photograph of your comrades reunited on a runway.

And this card, which brings you greetings
for a birthday close to Christmas –
Boats at Royan, Samuel John Peploe.
Will you remember kicking a ball on that beach,
eating frites around a table just beyond?

Now that your skin is a shammy,
you only feel sunlight through glass.
Or see the shapes it makes on walls
as it beckons behind a bolted door.

ON BEING SHUT OUT OF THE JARDIN DES POÈTES

The first snow that winter locked the gates,
closed in case of accidents on ice.

Through the fence, the mounds which hold
the plaques of verse faced away,
Hugo turned his monumental back.

Next door was officially closed,
but the gates were opened and I entered
the greenhouse garden – les Serres d'Auteuil.

An azalea held out purple next to bitten rhododendrons,
witch hazel wrote ochre in the snow,
a clipped box orb fell in with smooth grey stone.

A shrub, wrapped in a silver robe,
was tied at the waist, like a torso.

ELIZABETH TAYLOR'S NOSE

If these photographs were a pack of cards
I'd know how to lay them side by side in families.
Is this Queen with the floral frock
the mother of this baby?
Did this Jack of Hearts with his hand on the bonnet
of a Ford Anglia marry the girl in chiffon?
Had they moved to this white house
by the time photos came out in colour?

I've never seen anyone who looks like me,
not a mother or a brother or an aunt.
When I lay in my cot the staff touched my nose.
'Like Elizabeth Taylor's,' they said.
My name from them was Liz.

Chosen by new parents, to live in a solid house
on the borders – my name from them was Laura –
I shelled peas, broke off sticks of rhubarb,
learned to love mackerel.
I changed the date at school, defined the weather,
counted the petals on countless yellow daisies.
Academic work came easy.

With one birth certificate saying born in Scotland,
a second in Arbroath, I grabbed my passport.
My aeroplane flew low on a detour
from a foreign city, and there below in miniature –
the sheep and spinneys,
the drills and trellis of my Lanark home.

When there was enough life between I went looking –
too late to show my mother my content.
I read the cause of death –
heart attack at fifty.
I had her down for teenage pregnancy,

another family,
a possible half-sister or a brother.
At least a conversation where she could tell me
if this was Uncle Ted or Auntie Flo,
if this was really *her* covered in rose petals
from head to toe.

RETURNING HER WORDS TO MARY

The black doll you gave to me
turned green in the sun,
you stitched careful curtains
for a shoebox stage,
pull the string for magic.

You phone me about the rain,
put honey on your skin,
luxuriate in a bath of comfrey
wishing for a jacuzzi.

I find you sitting up asleep,
a shawl around your shoulders,
your cheeks an orange blaze.
I switch off the electric fire,
hold a candle to your face.
Live for the day and have a dream.

Wardrobes brim with distorted shoes,
three times round the market
for two pence off tomatoes,
bargains shunt through your shops, your home,
our homes, Oxfam.
I only know what I've got in my purse.

You could grow gladioli in gravel,
tiredness wipes you in the afternoon,
you wake nailed to the bed.
I want rubbing out and drawing again.

MEMENTO

In the place where the islanders
obey the speed limit,
where garage become hairdresser
becomes post office becomes store,
where the farmer's wife invites me for tea
in the house where the farmer was born,
You can't get more shiftless than that,
I have left a pair of shorts in the drawer,
I have left a pair of mint green silk shorts
in the second drawer down in the chest.

Where fulmars glide like balsa wood planes
over patches of glisten on the sea,
larks still their song over quilted hills,
buttercup, double poppy, moist green,
where the land is indented with water,
cows with pierced ears paddle lochs
or reply to the wails of the seals
on farms fenced down to the shore,

where dawn is intimate with dusk,
a place called Wilderness impossible to find,
where the farmer offers me drop scones
and three kinds of cake, where they once
lived in the cottage next door, newly wed,
where their son will live with his wife,
I have left silk shorts in the drawer
of the farmers who are afraid of large towns,
in the place where I am afraid of the cows.

THE GLASS MOUNTAIN

Perspex actually, pyramidal, built up
of smaller pyramids within,
each refracting light and holding a secret –
the shadow behind a waterfall,
the end of a story never told,
the first glass bead which flew from a broken necklace,
the terracotta plain which finished in a mountain.

Turned upside-down some objects stay in place –
an orang-utan pushing at his walls,
a section of mercury without air,
a scrap of light blue velvet;
the shadow behind the waterfall slips low,
the glass bead joins others from an earring,
the mountain unfolds to stretch along the grainy plain.

CORAL BEACH, LOCH DUNVEGAN

Bees zizz from left to right –
motorbikes accelerating in and out of earshot.

The round tablecloth of the sea is spread across the beach,
one scalloped edge after another.

The black head of a seal pushes through the surface of the water –
it turns like a periscope,
surveys the scene and disappears.

Wigs of ochre seaweed cover the skulls of rocks.

A feather bracelet dances in a jellyfish
as it advances with the lapping tide,
putting up no resistance.

Sifting through a ridge of broken shell and coral
I make a collection to whiten a windowsill.

GUTTED

These flats. I'm getting out of here.
I'm not going to be one of those they come round
collecting for wreaths for.

I want a room of my own.
Sean even gets hold of my underpants
if I don't watch him. And I'm sick of his City posters.

Telly's rubbish in the day. The adverts are alright.
I want to spear a dummy with a bayonet.
I bet my dad was in the army,
I bet he had boots and a gun.
I would stand to attention, I would
salute with my hand like this.

I wish I wasn't the eldest.
Sometimes I go to the fridge and drink
the baby's milk from her bottle.

THE WITHDRAWING ROOM

I am a medievalist but you can't sell cathedrals
and my husband has osteoporosis.
There are no right angles in this house
so rather than replicate the pargetting
the outside walls are smooth.
The National Trust replastered in 1984.

If you look through the cellar
there's evidence of the fifteenth century,
the mullions are turned at forty-five degrees.
When we came there were borders and flowers –
fiddly, and too grand for a farmhouse.
The Trust agreed and we planted weeping ash.

The entrance door has second phase supports,
with later scrolls and pediment –
a local carpenter who hadn't quite got the style.
Penrose unblocked the windows.
The oriel suggests *that* room was probably
a solar chamber, the withdrawing room.

Limed staircase, carved here with boring hearts and diamonds.
By the time he'd reached the top
he'd completely taken off.
I used to make polish.
Grate beeswax, turpentine and a good plain soap
like Fairy, to fill it out.
This is where I worked so hard on the panelling.
My son grew up in a wooden room.
Now he makes furniture.

I went to university the same year as my daughter.
She was a bit put out when I got a first,
we phoned each other every day.

I lived in one room with my dog.
When I came back I said I'm not doing anything,
you can do it for yourself.

The fireback is reproduction.
I thought no one will notice when it's covered in soot.
For a long time we thought the tiles were Dutch,
until a lady came from the V and A.
I mix the colours myself.
Contemporary designers find a beam
above a window very difficult.

In the summer I sleep on the second floor.
Oak floorboards were for servants
but they've lasted longer than the pine downstairs.
My mother is 88. I visit her every day.
She introduced me to her neighbour who is 106.
I put this mat down here. People slip.
I still must tidy my room.

CLEANING THE HOUSE, NAKED

At dawn she rises, fills a bowl with water,
bends to wipe the skirting board,
the walls are smeared with finger blood.

A tablecloth welcomes her scrubbing,
verdigris slides from the bend in a pan,
she leaves rooms drifting with lemon, myrrh, pine.

Her thighs are ribbed by the banister,
her back, a plain of cinnamon
catching pools of autumn light in the valley of her spine.

She lies down on the polished floor,
stretches her hands to smooth her belly,
thinks of a child she carried.

Her hair was apricot down,
her smile joined up countries
but her blood could not find a route through her heart.

They cradle each other together,
their skin slipping between absence,
the silt dropping from their innocent toes.

MAGNOLIA. BOTANICAL GARDENS, BATH

The fleshy pink petals competed with the clouds.
A crowd could sit beneath its blooms –
as a couple did, on a bench surrounded by fallen
petal hands beginning to bruise and brown.

It was one of many magnolias that day
which gleamed in the March sunlight,
white globes blushing pink from their stems.

Two women chatted on the path,
'*So disappointing for the rest of the year.*'
It cut me to the quick.
Does a day lily deserve such scorn?
Is it not worth making a baked Alaska?
Would one want a total eclipse every day of the year?
And if a child lives till the age of three,
seeing three springs, three summers, three falls,
does she not then shimmer through each winter?

ESTHER

I glide my hand over
her warm silk head,
the new hair stands
clear of her skin,
we rejoice in a tooth,
take turns to pat bottom,
we ponder the barrel of tummy,
laugh at her thighs
bulging like knotted balloons.

Her forehead frowns
as she makes sense of sunlight,
we reply to her sounds in sentences,
I am recognised with a smile.

When will she build a tower,
pedal a cycle, join a movement?
Her life will overlay ours.
She laces the present with future
with her one sock missing
and no liking for hats.

PORTHMINSTER BEACH

At first your mermaid was flat –
a line drawn round her wedge of tail,
fronds of thongweed for her hair,
her eyes two pokes of finger in the sand.

I made mine beside –
her belly swelled,
her breasts were easy cups inside my hand.
I left her swinging her hips
and rolling her bladderwrack eyes.

When I looked again
yours had grown two cones.
They stood proud for hours
before the high neap tide came in.

SMILE

My job is to make our baby smile.
I pulled the loose threads on her babygrow
till the two halves folded out
like the first in a line of paper dollies.
When her food drops into the lip of her bib
I put it back around her mouth.
If Mummy is gone a long time
I get her skin between my fingernails and squeeze.
Mummy thinks it's colic.
I hand her a nappy and unwind the lid on the cream.

If I keep smiling she should smile back.
I'm definitely more interesting than her toys –
what can you do with a rattle?
There is a book with pictures,
for *duck* I say *lorry*, for *cat – daffodil*.
I'm always banging into her cot when she's asleep
but I do smooth her forehead dome with my fingers
and sing about the wheels on that bus.
She grabs my thumb and grips as hard as she can.
I know she's going to smile soon – I can see it in her eyes.

'L'USAGE DE LA PAROLE,' MAGRITTE

(painting of stars which spell 'Désir')

This I think a particularly interesting constellation,
it can make an appearance late in autumn
when a sharp breeze hits the moist night air.
On one rare occasion it was visible
as the light dipped over a small North Sea fishing town.

The house was quiet,
stealth crept up the stairs,
garments were discarded,
holes were discovered in socks.
There was a distinct lack of formality.

By the time the light had lapsed to China blue,
the 'D' was over Orkney while the dot on the 'i'
tipped Tierra del Fuego further into the sea.

The formation has apparently realigned,
though further disturbances are anticipated.

CRAG PATH, ALDEBURGH

I've gone for a year without seeing you,
I've tried other coastlines,
been wooed by significant cliffs,
seething surf, the curve of a uterine bay.

You do not howl your attractions
but I always surge back – to see how the sea
pulls to the north but breaks to the south,
to watch the seal-grey horizon slip
behind the martello tower, to lie
on the wall in the company of gulls.

There are figures in this landscape –
evening and morning swimmers slide between
the hauled up fishing boats in cool September.
They chat a while, then slip their towelling gowns
and make no bones about it.
A triumphant red cap swims hard against the rutted water.

At night, when stars are pressed thickly into the sky
the fishermen will hunch behind umbrellas,
their lamps like cat's eyes plotting the line of the shore.

You are more constant than memory –
newspaper headlines billowing in the wind,
drinking cold coffee from a jade green cup,
a hasty kiss before the rain came down.

PLASTER DUST

I've had two dreams about this man,
he thinks he's welcome, in my sleep, to share my life.
We trolley down the aisles picking links of sausages,
a Sunday roast, I act the washing powder wife.

He's anxious in the second dream,
he can't make love. The walls suck in,
and now the carpet's full of come.
It curdles with the plaster dust from the ceiling rose above.

He holds me, sinks his head into my shoulder,
"Why does it have to be like this?" he moans.
The milk has risen to the armchair seat,
we oscillate our heads like whirring fans.

THE PIANO CAN BE LIMITING

if you want a tuba
which slides down towards the sea,

cymbals to clear the air of strings,
a piccolo pitched higher than a lark.

TAKING ALICE TO THE NEW BRITISH LIBRARY

Alice studied in the vast domed room in Bloomsbury on Saturdays,
in time spared from preparing students for exams.
She sat once in the wrong chair,
only realizing when she started adding to someone else's notes.
No chance now of sitting in the wrong chair
as we wheel her into lifts, along ramps,
between glass caskets of manuscripts and maps.

Now we wonder at a medieval world,
cerulean sea, golden mountain ranges
bunching like caterpillars –
all parallel and crawling East.
Unnamed rivers and deltas magnified
enough to flood the land,
lakes which look like guesses,
place names listed inside coastlines –
a tight fringe of landings.

North Africa is almost right,
Spain and France are true,
Asia melts south, indistinct,
like icing on a crystal cake.
The countries grow out of each other,
sharing frontiers, only Britain floats alone.

Alice would like a boat, but more than this a plane,
where she could sip chilled wine,
and plot hinterlands through the bleary window pane.

THE BRITISH MUSEUM PRINT ROOM

Van Gogh thought to be a preacher.
At twenty-one he came here and saw
the Rembrandt brown ink drawing over there,
then he did his own.

It lies in this glass case –
a splutter of rocks in the foreground,
a scruff of grass.
He drew every tree one behind the other
pulling right back to the horizon.

Dots become finer,
fields become thinner,
a track ripples to the right
while a train drags smoke to the left.

Stooks measure fields,
cypresses billow,
nothing is still.

SUNDAY MORNING

At one o'clock the shouting woke me,
Cunt, cunt, cunt.
I pushed it away, in need of sleep.
It was the breaking of glass
which brought me to the window,
and the scream of a child.

She stood in the doorway, back lit,
with a message for the street,
My Dad is hitting my Mum.
Blue lights revolved around my room,
an officer entered the house,
then another, then another.
The intervals were carefully timed.

A mother came into the doorway,
her baby bandaged in shawls.
I was backstage at a play,
the street waited behind a curtain.

The father was next to appear.
Held by the wrists and the feet
he swung like a dead pig
slung from a pole.
He was fed into the jaws of a van.

At midday I could hear the woman
hoovering glass in her front room.
She came to the window, looked up at the sky.
Rivers of rain slushed down the gutters.

THE TRAVELLING WARDROBE

for Rosie

Sometimes it stands in a desert –
waves of sand lapping over its feet.
It slips a tweed overcoat with a silk lining
over a dipping dune.

Sometimes it stands on a glacier,
one foot lodged in a crevasse.
The briefest of slips – satin edged voile –
slides from the half open door.

Sometimes it stands on a prairie,
waist high in chafing wheat.
Six pairs of white cotton baby socks
fly between the wind and the heat.

SPANISH DOLLS

They were attached at the back of their heads,
a twist of black wool sewn into their soft pink skulls –
cotton-covered flat-footed dancers
dangling from my fingers.

Her tiered flounces, white spots on red,
vied with his rufflette shirt,
his wide-brimmed felt black hat.
Her black boots ran half way up her calves,
both clutched polished castanets.
Their smiles were pushed sideways in stitches,

My white chest of drawers was wedged
across the corner of my room.
There they stood, in the company
of other couples – from Holland, France, Moldavia.

I left the Spaniards on a bus.

No amount of phone calls to Lost Property
turned them up. Their destiny –
to ride via Rochdale, Walmersley,
Ainsworth and Heap Bridge.
To fandango in the foothills of the Pennines,
jota between high-stacked market stalls,
seguidilla in the playground on a saint's day.

For holidays we went to Wales.
'Get to know your own country,' said Dad.

SANTA TERESA'S HAND

Knuckles stiff for centuries,
palm wrinkled like the skin of a dry lemon,
I lie on his bedside table crowded by
bottles of pills and wilting bougainvillaea
creeping from the window.

Morning and night my crystal box is brushed
by drapes of tassel and brocade.
He wakes and prays, places his hand over mine,
prays for a state of grace.

This man. Generalissimo. He thought to lift
unlike minds from his country
like so many beets from a field.
In the name of God he ripped the hands from children.
He wags a scythe at his people,
holds their fealty by a thumbtack.

I long for the apricot walls of Avila,
to trace the late shadows as they fall on the Sierra,
touch wet orange blossom by the fountain,
drizzle my fingers with hot candle wax.

I would stroke the necks of widows
at the back of gilded shrines,
smooth the folds from their knife thin shawls.

Franco kept one of Santa Teresa's mummified hands by his bedside.

IF YOU WERE HEADING FOR LONDON CITY AIRPORT, YOU'D BE FLYING BY NOW

(Hoarding, M4 approach road)

If you were making for Manchester,
you'd be lost by now,

If you were going to a garden,
you'd be smelling gardenias by now,

If you were heading for hospital,
you'd be giving birth by now,

If you were visiting your lover,
you'd be in bed by now.

If you were waiting at London City Airport,
you'd feel a hand on your shoulder by now,

If you were living in London city,
you'd be asked for money by now,

If you were driving to London,
you'd be hearing the Archers by now.

When you reach the garden,
you'll find it has been stripped by locusts.

INSTRUCTIONS, L'ULIVIERA

There is a window in the bathroom
which will steam over when you take a shower.
Only then will you realize it has slipped in its frame
to leave a strip of clear clay hills and russet roofs.

For two days you will rue the lack of towels.
The other side of the *arte povera* wardrobe
is opened with a tiny hidden hook.
The towels lie there quietly in deep and subtle piles.

The bed will bring the comfort of sleep
and the certainty in dreams
that your friends are capable of betrayal.

On the first night you will hear Italians banging and shouting
at the door in a necessary release of resentment
after years of thoughtless tourist parking.
You will, in fact, have left plenty of space
for the man and his wife to pass.

The woodburning stove will, in time,
warm the winter from the walls.

But as the pipe runs into the bedroom
it will scorch the sheets, the duvet and the mattress
while you are having wine, olives and conversation
with the couple from Norwich next door.

On the third day there will be sunshine,
on the fifth, snow.

TUSCAN MINIATURE

The sky is a staircase of duvets,
    a tent with cypress trees for props.
A pillow of trees embroidered in
    apricot and lime nestles in the valley.
The road licks round the hill
    like the tail of a lizard waiting in the lee.

THE BEAST AWAITS BEAUTY

My meal of straw and rose petals lies heavy,
there is a feather which has not reached the ground.
I can only ever hear the overture,
I peel the bark from switches,
I know a letter was sent to me.

She will come to me daily without warning.
She will be there when I lift my head,
knee-deep in michaelmas daisies.
We will smile with pleasure,
no need for a huge embrace.
She will bring me presents – an avocado,
a mandolin, a bee sting.

What did I do wrong?
The hills are thick with scorched stubble,
when my mother slipped and fell face down
I could do nothing for her.
I dreamt I died without love.

PSYCHE'S MOAN

It wasn't as if I was a shirker,
but the things she asked me to do…
I picked up the hairs from the salon floor,
graded them into sixteen braids –
colour, strength, length and curliness,
I did the eyelash tints for babies.
But could I re-wire the ancient yellow dryer?
(Gods know why she couldn't buy a new one,
she'd appointments end to end Monday to Saturday).

I asked at the Greek restaurant next door.
Perseus said it wasn't worth
a small round plate of stoned black olives.
So I tightened up the screws,
wiped it down with tulip oil
and hoped she wouldn't notice.
No one ever tried to use it.

The last task was dead easy –
replace the empty cans of hairspray
with new ones from the cellar.
There was a certain fragrance that she liked,
I didn't know its name.
It would take more than that to release me, I knew,
but I sprayed out each one in turn,
watched the fine film falling through the air,
and breathed in deeply.

It was Friday when they found me,
lying East to West on the cold cracked flags
clutching *Damask* in my hand.
Her face was white as a winter weasel.

FINDING DAVID IN THE LILIES

for Mabyn

You were repotting the orange lilies
when there was little left of your own life to arrange.
You ate well of our picnic – chicken livers, focaccia,

making more work for the canker.
Sitting in easy chairs we avoided the tyranny of the dinner table,
summer pudding for desert. I only ever made it for you,

it was *you* who usually did the giving of cakes.
You accepted my blooded shell of ruby berries and kept the remains.
Always there was conversation,

the best said of everyone, only details betrayed –
a cleric who arrived with his own camomile tea-bag,
neighbours who never received complaint.

At the end of the afternoon you showed your slides,
flicking between shots of Angela, Eileen, Karen.
Did you prefer Bronwen

with her hair slipping from her rolled turban,
or the second shot which showed her stamens full?
You decided on the first and referred back to your notes.

My garden and I have grown through you,
you would not let me stumble in my pronunciation of pelargonium.
I go to check the orange lilies – the pot you gave to me that day.

Their heads are wrapped in shawls of curling leaves.
I cup my hand to catch a falling beetle,
squash its hard red back

between my finger and my thumb.

LEATHERHEAD GEISHA

The down of her cheek greets me,
we repair to the sitting room
where arms of amaryllis leaves
stretch across the windows.

We run through parts of speech,
the uses of 'who' and 'whom',
the finer points of possession,
plurals apropos apostrophes.

Between each point we lift bone china to our lips,
sip broken orange pekoe,
replace the cup soundlessly
on the saucer's waiting palm.

Taking up where we last left off
we walk in the Garden of the Hesperides.
Her words are wound so well
I see reflections in Hera's golden apples,

I feel the vertebrae in Atlas's back
being squeezed towards the earth.
Before lunch, I learn to place a celandine
beside a burnet rose.

We eat on creamy linen,
slice pickled walnuts to eat with moons of tongue,
we replace the lids on tureens
to keep their heads of steam.

Conversation lifts and swells, gently,
like a spring tide of narratives
lapping towards the shore.
In the afternoon I lie for half an hour

on clean and ironed sheets,
lavender rubbed between the pillows.
I dream of a car alarm
with ever lengthening intervals.

A bath is waiting,
a towel is warmed,
I'm left to close the curtains,
as I wish.

Driving home
the motorway drives with rain,
cameras without film snag my gaining speed,
a lorry lies prostrate in a sodden ditch.

DREAMING OF A DEAD LOVER

Dead for fifteen years
he came to find me lying down –
he'd been busy in the kitchen.

Beneath the bedclothes,
the creamy renaissance folds,
he had a triple vision

which he wouldn't be without.
He didn't tell me what he saw
but held it to himself.

There was an ease,
which comes in sleep and stays.
In those moments he'd neither

jumped the slated roof
nor launched his car against
a winter tree.

His skin was smooth,
and delicate as pastry.

YALDING. 15TH OCTOBER 2000

On the village sign the Medway flows
safe within its swinging boundaries –
dark blue waves on a pale blue plane.
But on this Sunday afternoon

the residents are wearing rubber gloves,
their rooms have been removed –
left to dry in cold front gardens
where dahlias face the ground,

debris is caught up in shrubs,
carpets are piled like pancakes on a lawn.
The river, threaded through
with Chinese greens, is chicken stock;

the grass beside, flattened by the water's weight
is scabbed with newsprint, broken bottles,
a gaping plastic bin.
Outside the post office a single postcard

rests face down beside a shoal of rubber bands,
a camel train of sandbags stretches round the street.
While dampness rises half way up a house
a toy boat sails across an upstairs window.

A fallen garden wall, washed clean of pointing,
shows its gleaming terracotta bricks
and how they match the iris berries
in the seed head split behind.

A red winged armchair leans back on its legs
and laughs at the daylight.

THOUGHTS OF A MAN IN MAIDSTONE JAIL

I missed my daughter playing Juliet.
She showed me her new blazer the day I left,
there was Latin on the pocket.

I missed hickeys hiding under her poloneck,
the steamed up windows of a car outside,
lying in bed, waiting for our front door to slam.

My son draws row on row of railings sprouting leaves.
He asked if murder is in his genes,
'*Not unless you let it be,*' said his gentle mother.

She folds sheets for another man,
no mystery with him, no sleight of hand.
A jug of milk stands on the kitchen table.

I won't have them visit me,
they'll not bear the brunt of my mistake,
it's *my* four more years to do on twelve.

When I walk I may go back to Rawtenstall,
or on to Rochdale, I don't know.
Each way there'll be a rotten debt to pay.

ORNAMENTS

This room has seen a man immobile,
blocked into a chair for three days.
He didn't eat his double eggs for breakfast,
he didn't even read.

He came to score,
buggered off back to Boston
thrusting sixty dollars at his hostess.

She wouldn't have cared if he hadn't paid at all,
as long he removed his hire car
from the gravel sweep of her drive.

The wooden cockerels on the bookshelves
bowed their vermilion combs,
whispered to each other in worried tones.

Salmon has been secreted behind the beds,
great slabs of tuna, five swordfish,
a moist cheek of cod.

The Japanese visitors sat in running water,
used their hands as plates,
picked at flakes of halibut with their chopsticks.

The yellow ducks on the windowsill turned away
in mild ceramic disgust.

The honeymooners spilled confetti between the sheets,
lay across the single beds and melded into one.
Frost was twitching through the lavish lawns.

The geese on the opposite window giggled,
didn't know where to put themselves.

Meanwhile, next door, in the Queen Anne house,
the hostess lived in terror –
with a man sober enough to speak at ten o'clock.

He ranted after that, waking from his nap
to click the cabinet at six. She thinks
less and less of him now he's gone,
and wonders if his young Filipino dusts his ornaments.

IGUANA

I hadn't moved for days,
at night I simply put my feet up on the chair.
I would focus on one point in the garden –
the hole in the fence where a knot had been,
till all my muscles held a stillness born of strength.

At first my legs welded into one,
the green scales spread to yellow towards my thighs,
I rather liked the curl ending in my tail.

With feet the longest journey could begin.
I clutched the shelf-edge with my toes
and turned towards the painting on the wall.
Reflected on a mouth was *my* flabby crown,
my one black eye rested on his chin.
I ached to lick the surface of the paint,
to catch its roughness on my hoary tongue.
I envied the illusion of smoothness on his skin.

I will in time, of course, avoid the isolated tree.
Prehensile thought my tail may be
I'll choose the lower branches,
I'll listen out for moths,
and faces placed on pillows
in the surge of morning light.

DO YOU KNOW ORIGAMI?

At Alnmouth and Holy Island the train ran near the shore,
south of Berwick a knife levelled the sea to slate.

Opposite, a Glaswegian answered his mobile phone in patient tones,
beside me a Japanese girl folded paper.

Out of her fingers grew red cranes, pink swans,
green pointed balls made from twelve sheets of paper.

The swans grew cygnets – the size of a baby's thumbnail,
the fleet of cranes leaned on the table like grounded planes.

Her friend across the aisle was learning from a book,
she threw her first ball in the air and photographs were taken.

I read obituaries. Barbara Olson killed, American Airlines Flight 11.
She'd stayed on in Boston to breakfast with her husband on his birthday.

I could believe these lines of prose, a shocking three days later,
in their familiar place – the back of the morning paper.

I got back from the buffet to find the Glaswegian joining in.
He drew two black oval eyes on his nodding folded dog.

'*What will you do with them all?*' I asked the girl.
'*I am happy when I am making origami,*' came her reply.

Now her friend's neighbour was folding paper.
'*You've got competition,*' he said, eyeing the Glaswegian.

A steward came along the carriage collecting up the waste.
I yelped too late – he swept the surface of the table in his waiting sack.

'*Sorry,*' he said, picking out the larger birds.
'*No problem. I'll make some more.*'

The paper disappeared beneath her fingers,
another family hatched over the table.

She took a toffee from the Scottish lad and said,
'*Let's take over the world with origami.*'

ARCHANGEL

for Bryony

I am an elderly lady with a stammer,
my ears are long and slender,
I live in a chewing gum ball,
I live in a jacket in a shop,
I live in constant battle with my husband,
with two grandchildren who have never blinked since childhood.
Don't think I can't feel flies.

My daughter's doing sixteen months for theft –
I keep the keys of hailstones.
My mouth is ever open for birdspotting triumphs,
for twenty-three years I have smelt the spume of lorries,
I vie with my neighbours for vapours.

My life has been unremarkable,
I suck the rain from all-pink picnics.
In the early evening I walk the patrol –
peer in at windows.
I see electric fans, flicking screens,
silk flowers in dusty arrangements.
Allowed one flight a month
I used to leave sweeties on doorsteps.
Now I send letters of invitation –
to look at a lime tree,
or a ticket for a train on a circular route.
Wings came in useful once for planning treats.

On a very good day in July I tie Christmas baubles to the roof
and spew them out at passers-by.

A TABLE OF KINDRED AND AFFINITY

A woman may marry

a man who has eyes for kingfishers,
who leaves the lid on the casserole while the eggs scramble,
who can advise on the building of stagings,
who hides a piece of string in your luggage – you never know
    when you might need a piece of string,
who will take a machette to a bamboo tree to cut down a lever for the
    four wheel drive when it is stuck in a rut in the middle of the road,
who knows the names of five species of fungi,
who proposes on Dodman Point,
who knows the strength of button thread,
who gives you white peonies and his first Margaret Merril rose to
    bloom that summer tied with his folded paper bow,
who will hold a kidney bowl under your chin while you vomit,
who brings the speakers for his personal stereo to your hotel room,
who sprays your bed with eau de cologne to keep away mosquitoes,
a man who knows the limits of a mobile phone.

A man may marry

a woman with a liking for frogs,
who, while you are using her bathwater, dresses up with lipstick
    and high heels to propose on one knee when you appear in
    your towel on the landing,
who wants her obituary to read, *'she had a nice line in hats,'*
who wears a hat with paper violets while marinating brown trout
    with spring onions, five spices and ginger,
who knows that where there are geckoes there are no rats,
who knows the difference between the smell of vanilla in a young
    Sauvignon and Indian balsam on her fingers after popping
    seedheads by the river,

who gives presents sprinkled with gold metals stars which fall
    from the paper and lodge in your carpet for several years,
who pisses in your bottle of Paco Rabanne when you defect, albeit
    temporarily, to another woman,
who puts a feather in her hair to stalk herons,
a woman with a chair in her heart.

THE DAY BEFORE YESTERDAY

A horse doesn't know it has a forehead
until you smooth it with your hand.

Yesterday I closed my eyes at traffic lights
and remembered your arms.

Your hands stroked me a back,
your palms gave me shoulders,
your fingers left a new layer of skin.

And though our lips touched only twice
I swear you found a land within
                                    where colour grows.

ARMATURE

For the feet, I push against the scrim the fact
that we waited for each other in different bookshops.

With a knife I smooth the calves
with the thought of my Arran cardigan, newly washed,
folded over your battered brown briefcase
giving us the number 146 from the cloakroom.

At the knee is the confusion of the word lift with escalator.

The thighs I thumb with my fingers,
rub in the crazed brown paint
behind the furthest of Picasso's Dancers
with the blue impasto you noticed on the window.
It was then I wanted to slip my hand inside the warmth of yours.

The hips have got to be that wailing installation
reminding you of your first marriage –
a tortured face trapped beneath a sofa.

The torso will be the viewing platform –
the sun hitting the gold pinnacle of St Paul's,
the out of use Millennium Bridge you tried to use,
the wooden bollard bobbing in the water,
a quadrant of rainbow in a grey spotlit sky.
It was here I rediscovered your tallness,
my head inclined towards your shoulder.

The neck is a reference to a previous conversation.

The head will be the café.
'*You have the view,*' '*No, you have the view*',
'*Please, you have the view,*'
two vases of broad banana leaves,

a serviette laid over your knees for drinking tea,
the fineness of your opaline skin,
your exquisite finger ends,
the landscape of your pillow mouth my fingers mean to trace.

KEEMUN

I'm going to find a ghost writer
for my next set of poems –
someone with a hard hat on his shoulders,
no nails on his little toes,
a matter of webbing across both feet.

He'll sit down in April
among the red tulip spikes
in my garden and he'll have inspiration
to the tune of one a day
for a fortnight.

He'll know from the strength of the coffee
I give him what it is I want to say.
He'll know from the leaf of Keemun tea
floating in his afternoon cup
how I want it to end.

As for in between –
there's always the trickle of water
from the bottom of the plant pots
pooling up on the crazy paving
to give him a clue.

A PATH OF RICE

THE LIVING WAS EASY

There is a hammock strung between silver birch,
phlox bobbing beneath. I cannot see
men with testicles the size of gourds.
The breeze dries the blood on my legs
as it drips from my backside.
I climb in. Petals from a shot silk rose
fall and rest each on a raised mosquito bite.
I sleep, I do not dream.
For Hintock read Cuckfield, for Konyu read Slindon,
For Tarsau – Stunts Green, for Ban Pong – Framfield.

I wake. Hear bees sitting on lavender,
my eyes seize monbretia as they wave
across Canterbury bells.
Pap, laplap, four deaths a day,
Pap, laplap, soon on your way.
I tilt my face, soak the last afternoon rays,
stretch like a fox on the toolshed roof.

Damn this brightness, it scars my eyes,
the heat lacerates my brain leaving nothing.
I could be the lice let loose in the general's hut.
Where is Freddie's letter? Two years it took.
They said he could read it if he got out of bed.
What can I write to his wife? –
Address – No 2 Camp, Thailand?

And now Toosey tops it off nicely.
Sixteen months of lugging rocks for
the glory of a frigging emperor
and he thinks we might be horny?
He radioed to Delhi. Ten thousand

rubber johnnies floated from a plane –
like so many boxes of snowflakes.

It's my mind I want naked, like the white shoot
of a hidden hyacinth before it reaches the sun.

NO FURTHER

While I stand naked in the bamboo hut
I am my father. Our freckles fuse,
our noses redden, our hair bleaches to sand.

He is marching in the Arakan, his friends
fall at his feet, they die quietly –
Jamchapel (Honeychurch), Windy (Breeze), Oscar (Wild).

At seventy-four my father fights battles in his pyjamas.
He wakes on the floor of his room.
A Lancaster bomber painted on a china plate

climbs the frail wall.
He is marching, the sweat stands on his brow,
his nose glistens. His squadron seeps across

a tea-plantation, one man is invited in to bathe.
My father sits naked in a tin bath.
I ladle water over my shoulders,

come to welcome the knife of water down my back.
The scrubbing brush will not rid my feet of grime,
it lines my toenails like kohl.

Should I wash my hair first or my bucket of clothes?
The tin of water is mine, to dowse my sandals,
to dribble down my legs, to scald away the heat.

Outside, a soldier rests a gun
across his narrow shoulders.
He will patrol the camp tonight.

After nine I will go no further than my hut
with its woven walls and roof of folded leaves.

DID YOU ASK ME TO DANCE?

I know my way round my country,
I am reunited with familiarity,
there are five flowers on the prunus tree,
there's a possibility of scilla.
But I do not forget the banana palms,
the roses which flower in your country,
or the airport where Panasonic plant
seventeen televisions, English actors
extemporise behind the screen
in black tail coats and bonnets.
Fiona Shaw is dubbed in Thai.

I stepped onto the plane
with four minutes left to go.
How long did we drink in the Bull's Head,
Terminal 2, killing our Singha beer?
Did you ask me to dance?
I dance at forty thousand feet for you
and tamper with the cloud.

FAXING THROUGH THE NIGHT

While you are sleeping
the paper creeps through your machine,

it shudders and shakes,
curling towards

your bed cover,
whispering through the heat.

You sleep on.
I soak in a honey cream bath,

cook spaghetti with a new pancetta sauce,
watch the sun slip between the slated roofs

and lay down to sleep.
You are rising.

The paper lies on the floor
baring its words like a rib cage.

JUNGLE BOY – MAE SURIN, CAMP 5

Mie Tha smiles and peacocks open their tails.

Mie Tha pours a bucket over his head
and the river changes direction.

Mie Tha tells a story of rape and death
and a Prussian blue touches his shoulder.

Mie Tha strokes a spray of paddy
and it yields a path of rice over the mountains.

WAITING FOR THE NIGHT

I have followed the sun around the balcony,
watched out of focus rainbows in my hair,
the sky throwing pocket sunsets behind steel clouds.
I have painted my toenails rose.

I am the shiny green tiles sliding down the temple roof,
I am the sprays of bananas on the moving cart,
I am the white citadel perched on the risen tower.

I am the river – Chao Phraya, Chao Phraya, Chao Phraya.
I lie under the belly of a wooden arc,
I drench the curve of a longboat,
I spray the lenses of cameras.
My vapour glosses the Gulf of Siam.

GUAN YIN AT ZHONG QIOU JIE

I couldn't find the right god
so I went to the nearest.
She lay in labyrinthine sois
surrounded by stacks of soap, toothpaste,
mooncakes, iced cakes, oranges,
incense, candles, bananas,
rice, orchids, ticking lights.

The Bangkok Post said the Chinese
didn't bother any more but they were wrong.
Home after home had its altar,
Men bowed with bunches of burning incense
offering up their prayers.

Then there was fire. Fire for mercy,
fire for beauty, fire for good business –
charred gold folded card,
melting magenta tissue paper
in burning metal bins.

Have mercy on my soul –
that I may never doubt that I am loved.

Have mercy on his soul –
for he wants to kill five businessmen
from five countries and then to kill himself.

Have mercy on their souls –
for striking out a nation like so many matchsticks.

TAKING AWAY TATTOOS

Aung Than Lay used pigskin.
He lay it over the navy dye,
over the symbol which means nothing,
till his forearm was bleached and the smell set in.
The ink stayed in his skin.

My father used a box of matches.
In a pre-nuptial ritual he singed his ginger hair
and seared his skin to a scar.
The blue and red veins surfaced
like a circuit.

Both men wanting to be like their friends –
in the French air force,
in the British air force.
My father's arm fair and freckled
carries the memory of a sword and a snake.
Aung Than lay's arm, brown
as the river in the rainy season,
still carries a gun.

Aung Than Lay is the outgoing Prime Minister of the
Karenni National Progressive Party.

WHEN THE REVOLUTIONARY GAVE UP HIS ROOM

I slept with the blood of an urban warrior –
his spine a twist of barley sugar,
his foot wrenching at uneven ground,
his shoulder weighing against the river taxi rail,
his arm leaking whisky over the injured on the bus.

As I lay on his bed of matting and tartan rugs
the aeroplanes flew low,
his watch flashed blue to signal sleep,
the blood clung to the mosquito net
like rubies falling through gauze.

When I awoke my face was smudged with red,
there were splinters of bone between my toes.
I turned – a gash sliced my side,
a bullet came to rest on the pillow.
My fingernails had been replaced
with petals from a wilting rose.

MV PANDAW RIVER JOURNEYS

Delighted to offer a series of journeys aboard
a refurbished 1940s paddle steamer.
A former British colony of geographical variety and natural beauty.
I will do what I like.

Even the most seasoned traveller will find himself in a world
that is beyond both experience and imagination.
One million people have been displaced inside the country,
800,000 refugees have fled.
A former British colony naturally betrayed and geographically
        isolated.
No one has suggested I stop operating there.

The centrality of the rivers is most convenient for the traveller,
both ancient sites and areas of contemporary life situated close to
        their banks.
Forced labour has been used to restore some of the tourist sites
including Mandalay Palace, also to upgrade railways, roads
        and airports.
If the work site is far from their village
people sleep by the side of the road, neither shelter nor water.
In some cases, women who are forced to stay overnight
can be raped by army officers.

Totally refurbished, yet conserving many of its original fea-
tures,
the pre-war colonial style Pandaw
is a quintessential part of the Irrawaddy experience.
Cabin windows have insect netting fixed
so windows may be kept open in preference to air-conditioning.
Broad promenade decks form a place to rest
and reflect on the passing riverscape.
I have no personal evidence.
My sources are confidential.

Briefings are held each evening when our guide will be available
   for discussion,
these are usually lively and enjoyable occasions.
Those involved in forced labour are required to provide their own
   tools and food.
As one refugee who escaped to Thailand said,
'I contributed labour, food, medicine and tools.
All the military gave was orders.'
Tourism is not a political issue.
I take full responsibility for any adverse publicity.
I will not pull out of Burma.

Transportation and accommodation combine with good food and
   drink to ensure a
tranquil yet stimulating insight into the hidden Burma.
Fly from Rangoon back to London via Bangkok.
I get pleasure from my business.
I will not pull out of Burma.
Your travels need not end here,
we can arrange beach extensions and onward travel
further into South East Asia.

MEET ME HALF WAY

There are many ways I could meet you –
half way down a flight of stairs carpeted in red,
in a dense departure lounge,
towards the end of an unlit government corridor.

A loading bay, dodging piles of cargo,
peeping over stacks of boxes stamped in blue –
Cape, Mauritius, Rajasthan.
Careful underfoot – there may be
treacle slicks of oil reflecting midday sun.

Some meetings will be pre-arranged,
some pure accident.
Our heads might come together
over three inch iris on the garden path –
a comment on their markings,
the way the orange flash reaches to the wall.

You could click your heels – the way you did
at River City, in the military way.
Though that was in farewell.
Before I can think of that, I want to meet you
in my passenger seat,
in my bathroom,
in the twisted hall.
Anywhere there's darkness,
where a new garment could easily fall.

THE BORROWED HOUSE

Back at home the blue stain from the candle wax
has washed clean out of the tablecloth,
the flowers you picked for the table
are topping off the compost,
(will you ever need that lesson again
in how to eat spaghetti?)
the log you upended to smoulder
for charcoal is still lying in the grate.

Here, three counties from my home,
in this borrowed house, the iris bloom
which should have shown before you left.
Slowly they unfurl, turning from a May Day fire,
leaning from the vase at half their usual height.
They're old as well as new.
Without an upright stance
their heads stoop towards the walls,
I fear the lower buds may never flower.

It took coming here to realize the last few weeks –
the drive through rape fields, the wide horizons,
the waking in a place you have not been.
No longer do I crave your daily voice,
my memory loosens to bring me evidence –
the origin of a tie pin,
welcome snores at the beginning of the night,
a lark you believed to be there,
a brother dying in your arms,
the construction of crockery on the drainer
when you did the washing up,
'I don't want to be a guest right from the start.'

This, I shall paint into the present, and this –
a picture of you naked, miming.
The scene – a prison room, the officers are sitting down.
You act the part of a detainee, you're told to

bend your knees, stretch your arms,
as if sitting astride a motorbike.
You must make your body shudder with the rumble of the engine.
As you play out for me this torture from inside Insein jail
flames from the hearth mark you out in gold.
'We had to stay like this for hours.'

CHRISSIE GITTINS was born in Bury in Lancashire. After studying at Newcastle University she took a Fine Art degree at St Martin's in London, and worked as an artist and a teacher before becoming a full-time freelance writer.

She has published two pamphlet collections of poetry with Dagger Press – *A Path of Rice* and *Pilot*. She has won prizes in the Lancaster Literature Festival Poetry Competition, *Poetry News* competitions, the Yorkshire Open and the Ottakar's Faber Poetry Competition. Her poems, short stories and poems for children have appeared in a wide range of magazines, newspapers and anthologies; several have been broadcast on BBC Radio Four and on the BBC World Service. Her children's poems won two prizes in the 2002 Belmont Poetry Prize and her children's collection *Now You See Me, Now You...* was shortlisted for the CLPE Poetry Award 2003. She also writes plays for BBC Radio Four.

She has held residencies at Springhill Hospice Rochdale, Bangkok Patana School Thailand and Belmarsh Prison Thamesmead and in 2001 she was awarded an international fellowship at Hawthornden Castle.